Ev

I

CW01433079

The Top News
Stories of the Year

By Hugh Morrison

Montpelier Publishing
London

ISBN-13: 978-1547211838
ISBN-10: 1547211830

Published by Montpelier Publishing, London.
Printed and distributed by Amazon Createspace.

Events of
1977

The death penalty is back

First execution in the USA since 1967

Dominus vobiscum – the Lord be with you – were the last words of Gary Gilmore (1940-1977) to his prison chaplain as he became the first person to be executed in the USA since the death penalty was suspended in 1967.

In July 1976 Gilmore, a habitual criminal, shot and killed two men in Utah in cold blood while robbing them, despite them offering no resistance. A witness noted Gilmore's vehicle licence number and he was soon arrested. A Utah jury unanimously found him guilty and due to the heinous nature of the crime, recommended the death penalty. Despite several stays of execution after protests from civil liberties groups, Gilmore did not attempt to fight the decision and accepted the verdict of the court.

Concerned that a hanging might be botched, Gilmore opted to be shot by a firing squad instead, and was duly executed on 17 January 1977 at Utah State Prison. The case caused a media sensation and a novel by Norman Mailer based on Gilmore's life, *The Executioner's Song*, was published in 1979.

Anarchy in the UK

The Sex Pistols hit the headlines

Punk band the Sex Pistols had already caused a national outcry when they engaged in a foul-mouthed exchange with presenter Bill Grundy on ITV's *Today* programme in December 1976.

In January 1977 the band hit the headlines again as their record company EMI sacked them, partly due to refusal by EMI staff to handle their records because of obscene content and because of alleged bad behaviour by the group on tour in Holland. Later in the year the Pistols were signed to Virgin Records but again sacked, largely due to complaints about their anti-establishment record *God Save the Queen,* with London's Conservative councillor Bernard Brook-Partridge describing the group as 'unbelievably nauseating'.

Further incidents of violence and protests dogged the band, particularly after guitarist Sid Vicious joined, and the Pistols began their slide towards break-up, which occurred in January 1978.

Aniefo Nationaal Archief

Snow in the Sunshine State

First recorded snowfall in Palm Beach

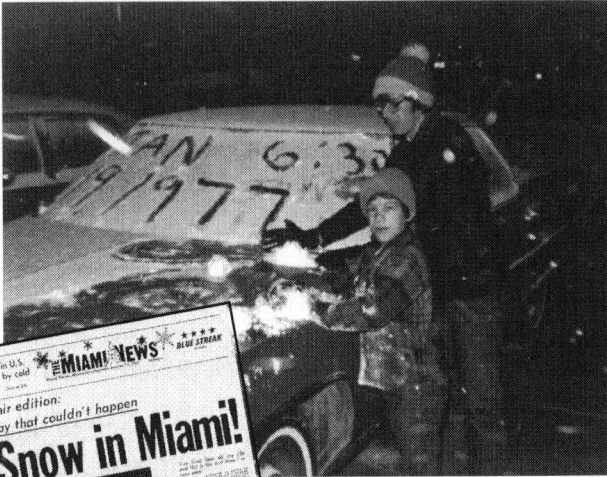

Tampapix

West Palm Beach in Miami, Florida, is not the kind of place you expect to find snow. But on 19 January 1977, residents woke up to find the 'impossible' had happened – their normally sun-drenched resort was coated with snow drifts of up to three inches in places.

Although there had been previous snowfalls in northern Florida, with one particularly memorable blizzard at Jacksonville in 1899, there had never been recorded snowfall this far south. Snow was even seen at Homestead in the far south of mainland Florida. Newspapers reported the event with headlines of the size usually reserved for the outbreak of war, with the *Miami News* announcing it as 'The Day That Couldn't Happen.'

Whilst it was a brief novelty for most Florida residents, the historic snowfall caused considerable damage to the state's delicate tropical food crops.

Fortunately no equivalent blizzard has since returned to Miami and the city continues to enjoy its reputation as an all-year-round hotspot.

Victory for Jimmy Carter

New president takes over from Gerald Ford

Jimmy Carter (born 1924) became the 39th President of the United States on 20 January 1977. The previous administration, under Richard Nixon and then Gerald Ford, had been dogged by scandal, and the USA was in the midst of a recession and oil crisis.

Carter was realistic about his prospects, saying in his inaugural address 'We have learned that more is not necessarily better, that even our great nation has its recognised limits, and that we can neither answer all questions nor solve all problems.'

One of his first acts as President, on his second day in office, was to declare an amnesty for those who had evaded the draft (military service) during the Vietnam War.

In 1977 Carter oversaw a number of social reforms such as the Federal Mine Safety and Health Act, and established two new federal departments, the Department of Energy and the Department of Education.

Having worked previously as a farmer, and being the only President to have lived in social housing, Carter was seen as something of an 'outsider', and ran into trouble with Congress when opposing 'pork barrel' public spending projects that seemed designed to bring money into specific representatives' districts.

Carter was defeated by Ronald Reagan in a landslide victory in 1980. He currently holds the record for the longest-retired President.

Black America finds its *Roots*

TV miniseries becomes surprise smash hit

LeVar Burton played Kunte Kinte in *Roots*

Only a few years after the last racial segregation laws were repealed in the US, the history of America's black population was still a highly sensitive subject in the 1970s.

Small wonder then that executives at ABC-TV had apprehensions about airing a new miniseries, *Roots,* based on Alex Haley's novel *Roots: the Saga of an American Family.*

They need not have worried. The series became a smash hit, watched by 140 million viewers, approximately half the population of the USA, the highest ever viewing figures in US history.

The series tells the story of a family from 1750 to the aftermath of the American Civil War, beginning with Kunte Kinte (LeVar Burton) being taken as a slave from Africa to the American colonies and ends with his descendant, 'Chicken George' (Ben Vereen) starting a new life in Tennessee as a freed slave in the 1870s.

The show involved a number of well known actors, including George Hamilton, Jeff Bridges and Burl Ives, as well novelist Maya Angelou in a supporting role.

The series was followed by a sequel, *Roots: the Next Generation,* in 1979.

A salute to *Salyut 6*

New Russian space station launched

Above: a test version of *Salyut 6* on display in Russia.

Russia's *Salyut 6* space station, launched on 29 September 1977, was a revolutionary new design that was a step towards the goal of permanent manned space stations.

Previous orbital space stations had not been able to take on board new supplies or dispose of waste, limiting the time that cosmonauts could live on board to three months. Salyut 6 however featured docking ports which allowed relief craft to resupply, change over personnel and dispose of waste.

This enabled crews to live for indefinite periods on board, with the longest *Salyut 6* mission lasting 185 days.

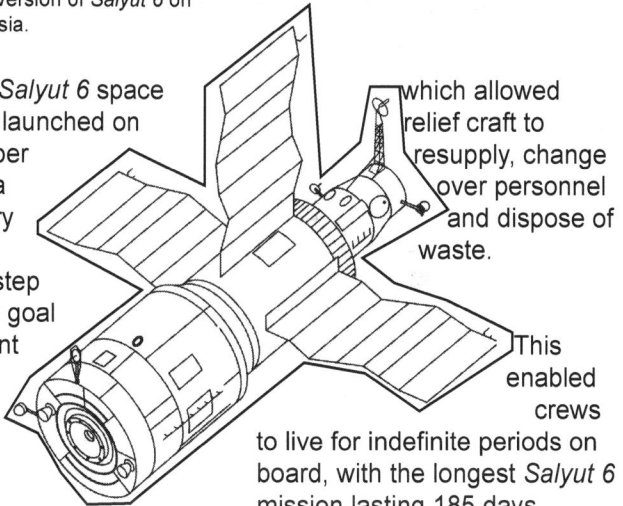

The main duties of the space station were astronomy, earth resources observation and the study of the effect of space flight on the human body. The station was in use until 1982.

Morph takes shape

Forerunner of *Wallace and Gromit*

Giles Farrington

Wallace and Gromit, the plasticine animated stars of films such as *The Wrong Trousers* are now world famous.

Aardman Animations, the company that created them, honed their skills many years earlier with a slightly more simple but equally loveable character: Morph.

The clay stop-motion animation was created in 1977 for BBC children's art series *Take Hart*, presented by Tony Hart.

Morph's name was taken from his ability to change shape, and he was able to become a ball and roll around, or extrude into a cylinder to pass through horizontal or vertical surfaces. He was also able to mimic other objects and creatures.

Inhabiting a box on Tony Hart's desk he would interact with the presenter in short sequences during the programme, using a gobblydedgook language which nonetheless Hart seemed to understand.

Morph, later joined by other characters such as Chas and Foily, went on to appear in various programmes over the years, and in 2015 Aardman Productions launched 15 new episodes of *Morph*.

Enterprise hitches a ride

First test flight for the Space Shuttle

NASA had been developing a reusable space craft since 1972, intended for use in constructing space stations and launching satellites, as a far cheaper alternative to disposable rockets.

By 1977 they had developed a workable prototype, *Enterprise*, named after the ship in TV series *Star Trek* following a massive letter writing campaign to NASA by fans of the show.

This was a high altitude glider to be used for landing tests known as the ALT (Approach and Landing Tests) programme. It first flew on the back of a modified Boeing 747 aeroplane on 18 February 1977, and following successful tests it was launched with a crew, again from the back of a jet plane, on 12 August 1977.

Although the shuttle did not have functional engines or heat shields, the crew were able to successfully glide to its landing site.

Enterprise was retired in 1979 after the conclusion of the the ALT programme. It provided valuable information for the construction of the first space-going shuttle, *Columbia*, launched in 1981. The last space shuttle mission took place in 2011.

Bette Davis

Lifetime Achievement Award for Hollywood star

Veteran Hollywood star Bette Davis (1908-1989) became, in 1977, the first woman to receive the American Film Institute's Lifetime Achievement Award.

The award was established by the Board of Directors of the American Film Institute in 1973 to honour a single individual for his or her lifetime contribution to enriching American culture through motion pictures and television.

Regarded by many as one of the greatest stars of Hollywood's golden era, Bette Davis began her movie career in 1930 and continued acting until her death in 1989. Some of her hits included *Now Voyager* and *Whatever Happened to Baby Jane?*

Davis' contribution to cinema was huge, and unlike many actresses she successfully made the transition from young starlet to mature performer.

Alan Light

Queen of Australia

Her Majesty opens Parliament

The Queen arrives at Brisbane (left) and opens Parliament in Canberra (right, with Prince Philip).

Although King George VI visited Australia when Duke of York, Queen Elizabeth II is the only reigning monarch to have visited the realm.

During her extended Australian tour in her Silver Jubilee year of 1977, the Queen was able to make history by becoming the first sovereign to open Parliament.

The Queen opens the British parliament once a year, but in Australia this ceremonial duty is carried out by the Governor-General acting on the sovereign's behalf.

The event was a chance to shore up popularity for the monarchy in Australia following its constitutional crisis in late 1975, when Governor-General Sir John Kerr controversially used his powers as the Queen's representative (the Royal Prerogative) to dissolve (close) Australia's parliament. This had not happened in Britain itself since 1831.

If the visit was intended to improve the monarchy's image, it worked: the Queen and Prince Philip were greeted by enthusiastic crowds wherever they went.

Rings of Uranus discovered

18th century theory proved right

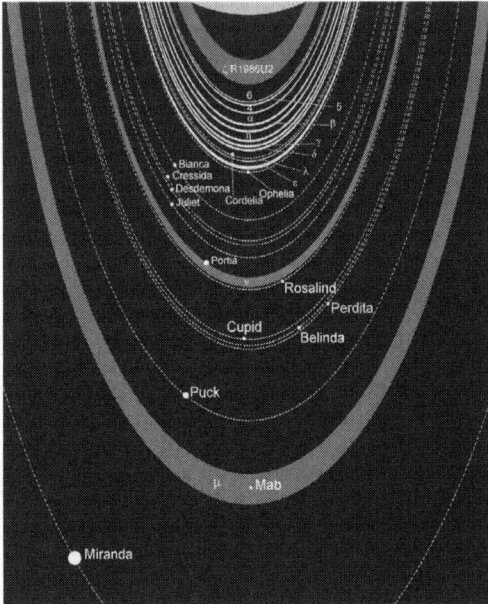

The system of rings and trace rings around Uranus

Although astronomer William Herschel suspected as long ago as 1789 that the seventh planet, Uranus, had rings, positive proof was not found until 10 March 1977.

Astronomers James L. Elliot, Edward W. Dunham, and Jessica Mink made the discovert by chance using the Kuiper Airborne Observatory (an aeroplane fitted with telescopes). They noticed that a star beyond the planet frequently became obscured, which led them to deduce that nine rings were orbiting the planet.

They were proved correct in 1986 when the Voyager space probe photographed eleven rings, comprised mainly of dust and ice. A further two rings were discovered by 2005 by astronomers using the Hubble Space Telescope.

Centenary of Test Cricket

Commemorative match in Australia

The first Test Cricket match between England and Australia took place in 1877, with Australia winning after England was bowled out for 108. Thus began a tradition of annual Test Cricket between various nations mostly of the British Commonwealth.

To celebrate the centenary of this momentous occasion in the sport, a special match was

Below: the 1877 England team. Far right: 1977 England captain Tony Greig. Right: Australian fast bowler Dennis Lillee MBE.

played between England and Australia in Melbourne from 12 to 17 March 1977.

The Australians were captained by GS Chappell and the English by AW Greig, with the Australian side including legendary fast bowler Dennis Lillee. Australia won the match by 45 runs.

End of an icon

Rover rolls out the last P6

The last Rover P6, now at Gaydon Heritage Motor Centre

Roverp6man

The Rover P6 series, known as the Rover 2000, 2200 or 3500 depending on engine, was a fast and agile saloon produced by Rover (later part of the British Leyland group) from 1963 to 1977. In 1964 it won the Car of the Year Award, the first to receive the accolade.

The car was designed to bridge the gap between small 1.5 litre saloons and the larger, expensive 3 litre cars such as the Wolseley 6. It was originally designed to be fitted with a Rover gas turbine engine but in the end these did not go into production. It did however feature a number of innovative technical details such as synchromesh gears, disc brakes and tube suspension. American models included power steering, air conditioning and electric windows, although the car never achieved popularity with the US market.

It is probably best remembered as a police area or squad car used by various forces in the UK, superceding the Wolseley 6, one of the first to use the 'jam sandwich' white and red livery.

Tragedy in Tenerife

583 killed in worst ever aeroplane crash

The deadliest accident in aviation history took place on 27 March 1977 on the island of Tenerife, one of Spain's Canary Islands, when two Boeing 747 passenger jets collided on the runway at Los Rodeos airport.

Following a bomb explosion at the airport on the neighbouring island of Gran Canaria, flights were diverted to Tenerife. As a result of congestion many aircraft had to park on the runway, considerably reducing visibility. A dense fog further worsened the situation. As two aircraft attempted to get into position for takeoff, visual contact with the control tower was lost and neither plane could see the other. In the resulting collision all 248 passengers and crew on one plane, belonging to Dutch airline KLM, were killed. The other plane, from America's Pan Am, suffered 335 fatalities, with 61 survivors.

The disaster had lasting effects on the aviation industry, with standardised phraseology adopted by air traffic control to avoid misunderstandings, and junior crew members being encouraged to question orders which they did not believe were correct.

The KLM Boeing on which 248 were killed. Inset: the memorial to the victims in Amsterdam.

TENERIFE 27 MAART 1977

KLM

Clipperarctic

Anyone for Demis?

Abigail's Party premieres in London

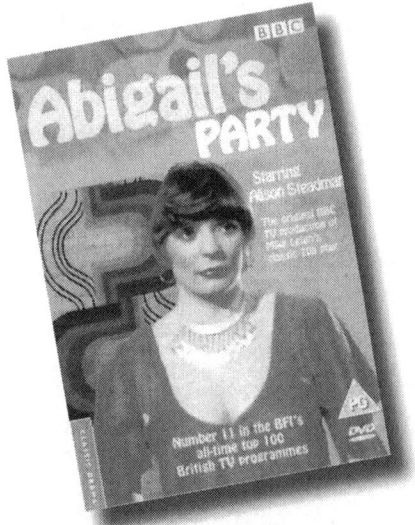

Mike Leigh's comedy of suburban manners, *Abigail's Party*, was one of the smash theatre hits of 1977 with an equally popular TV version.

The play satirised the worst aspects of 1970s social climbing and lower-middle-class pretensions with star performances from Alison Steadman, Janine Duvitski and John Salthouse. The play was a sell out at the Hampstead Theatre in London with 104 performances and was later filmed for BBC's *Play for Today*.

The action takes place in a suburban sitting room on the eastern borders of London, where hostess Beverley (Alison Steadman) forcibly entertains her guests with a steady stream of attempts at one-upmanship, as well as belittling her husband and forcing him to listen to music by Demis Roussos.

The play builds to a dramatic conclusion but we never actually see the eponymous Abigail, who turns out to be a teenager holding a party in another house. Some of the play's memorable lines include:

He's not violent, he's just a bit nasty. Like the other day he said he'd like to sellotape my mouth.

We don't want to listen to that fat Greek caterwauling all night.

Laurence, we're not here to hold conversations, we're here to enjoy ourselves.

Have you ever tried pilchard curry?

The 'funniest ever film'

Annie Hall wins critical acclaim

Woody Allen's romantic comedy *Annie Hall* was one of the smash cinema hits of 1977. Set in New York City, the film tells the story of the relationship between comedian Alvie Singer (Woody Allen) and Annie Hall (Diane Keaton).

The couple move in together and all goes well at first but eventually the relationship breaks down and the film looks back on what went wrong, both in Alvie's life with Annie and with his former lovers.

The film will be familiar to fans of Woody Allen with its themes of neurosis, Jewish identity, psychotherapy, and the lives of New York's artistic/intellectual set. Departing from cinematic convention, Allen breaks the 'fourth wall' and addresses the audience directly, and a similar scene occurs when the couple are queuing to see a film and overhear an argument between two men about the work of writer Marshall McLuhan. McLuhan himself then steps forward from his place in the queue to set the matter straight.

Although some critics disliked the film as being unfunny and self indulgent, Annie Hall was met with widespread critical acclaim on its release.

The film won four Oscars and was nominated for five, although it was beaten in the Best Picture category by *Rocky*. In the British Academy of Film and Television Arts (BAFTA) Awards it won Best Film. The Writers' Guild of America went further, and declared it the 'funniest ever film' in its list of 101 top comedies.

End of a legend

Bobby Moore plays last game in England

Bobby Moore OBE (1941-1993) made his final professional association football appearance in England on 14 May 1977, playing for Fulham against Blackburn Rovers.

The star player, described by Pelé as the best defender he had ever played against, began his career with West Ham, although he also played county cricket for Essex on the youth team. He was called up to the England squad during the 1960 World Cup and in 1963 became, at 22, the youngest player to captain England, in a 4-2 victory against Czechoslovakia.

Moore's finest hour, of course, was as captain of the victorious England team in the 1966 World Cup. After his final game in England, Moore played briefly for teams in the USA and Sweden and went on to become manager of Southend United.

After his death he was honoured with a memorial service in Westminster Abbey, one of only two sportsmen in history to receive this accolade.

'In a galaxy far, far away...'

Star Wars hits the screens

Star Wars was released in the USA on 25 May 1977 and rapidly became one of the highest grossing and popular films in cinema history.

From the moment the rolling credits began, with their famous opening lines of 'A long time ago in a galaxy far, far away' audiences were gripped.

Written and directed by George Lucas, the film tells the story of Rebel Alliance, led by Princess Leia (Carrie Fisher), and its attempt to destroy the Galactic Empire's space station, the Death Star. Farmhand Luke Skywalker (Mark Hamill) is drawn into the conflict when he inadvertently acquires a pair of droids with stolen plans of the Death Star. Skywalker accompanies Jedi Master Obi-Wan Kenobi (Alec Guinness) on a mission to return the plans to the Rebel Alliance and rescue Princess Leia from the clutches of the evil Darth Vader.

A distinguishing feature of *Star Wars* was its special effects.

Highly realistic models were used, but instead of attempting to move the models, as was done in earlier sci-fi films, the camera itself was moved rapidly towards static models to give the illusion of movement.

Lucas also employed the concept of 'used future', where space craft, costumes etc all looked worn, grimy and lived-in rather than shiny and spotless as in many other films. This added an extra dimension of realism.

Long to reign over us

Queen celebrates Silver Jubilee

In 1977 Britain and the Commonwealth celebrated twenty five years since the accession to the throne of Queen Elizabeth II. The celebrations began with church services on 6 February, the date in 1952 when Princess Elizabeth became Queen after the sudden death of her father, King George VI.

In June, huge celebrations took place across the United Kingdom with street parties, parades and firework displays. A chain of beacons was lit across the country and the Queen travelled by barge along the Thames in the route taken by her predecessor, Elizabeth I.

The year also included state visits to many Commonwealth countries, including Australia, New Zealand and Canada, in which three countries the Queen also presided over the state opening of parliament.

Below: a street party in Plymouth.
Right: a commemorative stamp.

SILVER JUBILEE
E R
1952 9P 1977

Steve Johnson

Hunt for a killer

Was Martin Luther King's assassin helped to escape?

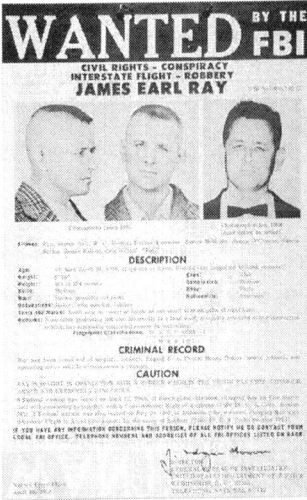

James Earl Ray (1928-1998) was convicted of the assassination of civil rights campaigner and clergyman Dr Martin Luther King Jr in 1968 and the following year was sentenced to 99 years in prison.

On 10 June 1977 Ray and six other convicts escaped from Brushy Mountain State Penitentiary in Petros, Tennessee. A three day manhunt by the FBI ensued and the group were recaptured. The escape rekindled speculation that Ray had been involved in some sort of conspiracy. Although Ray had confessed to killing King, he later retracted this, claiming that a shadowy figure known only as 'Raul' had been involved in the killing.

Ray's attorney Jack Kershaw claimed the escape suggested Ray had outside assistance. In 1997, a restaurant owner, Loyd Jowers alleged in court that the police had carried out the killing, but the case was thrown out due to a lack of evidence.

One man, no vote

Spain holds first election since Franco's death

General Francisco Franco ruled as the dictator of Spain from 1936 until 1975, during which no elections were held. Following Franco's death, the monarchy was restored under King Juan Carlos and Spain began a two year transition to democracy.

With the memory of the country's bloody civil war (1936-39) still relatively fresh, the transition was difficult, with many on the left unwilling to trust a monarch, even a constitutional one, who owed his position to a dictator.

Although marred by demonstrations and some outbreaks of violence, the country's first free elections on 15 June 1977 were carried out largely peacefully, with the Union of the Democratic Centre Party victorious, headed by Adolfo Suárez.

Top: General Franco. Below. Adolfo Suárez González, Duke of Suárez, Spain's first democratically elected Prime Minister. Below. HM King Juan Carlos I.

Brezhnev takes over

Russia's top man secures position

Leonid Brezhnev (1906-1982) took over as leader of the Soviet Union in 1977. He joined the Communist Party at a young age and survived the purges of Stalin as well as the Second World War, in which he served as a political commissar on the Ukranian front, ending up as part of the occupying army in Prague in 1945.

His rise through the political ranks post-war was rapid, as he was favoured by Stalin and later Kruschev; by 1960 he had become Chairman of the Presidium of the Supreme Soviet, the nominal head of state. Real power however rested with Kruschev, but he was ousted in 1964 as a result of a political plot.

Possibly having been involved in the plot, Brezhnev took over as General Secretary of the Communist Party. Only one man stood in his way to absolute power – Nikolai Podgorny, Chairman of the Supreme Soviet. In 1977 Podgorny too was removed, and Brezhnev ruled until his death, the longest term of any Soviet leader besides Stalin.

New York goes dark

City-wide blackout leads to looting and arson

At 8.37pm on 13 July 1977, lightning struck an electricity substation in New York, followed by two further strikes on other parts of the system, leading to a blackout of almost the entire city.

The city was plunged into darkness, airports were closed, and 4,000 people had to be evacuated from the city's subway system. Then came the looting and arson; gangs used cars to smash shop windows and many buildings were set on fire. 3,776 people were detained in the largest mass arrest in the city's history, with suspects put into chain gangs and held in makeshift holding pens due to lack of jail space.

A similar blackout had occurred in 1965, and would occur again in 2003. In both of those events the citizens of New York behaved, by and large, very well and many even remarked on how the blackout brought people closer together. In 1977 by contrast New York was in the midst of a financial crisis and the blackout may have brought out many of the city's existing problems.

Power was not fully restored until late the next day. Afterwards the electricity companies introduced measures to prevent a similar blackout occurring again; the 2003 outage was caused by problems in Ohio rather than New York.

Bond is back!

007 hits the screens again

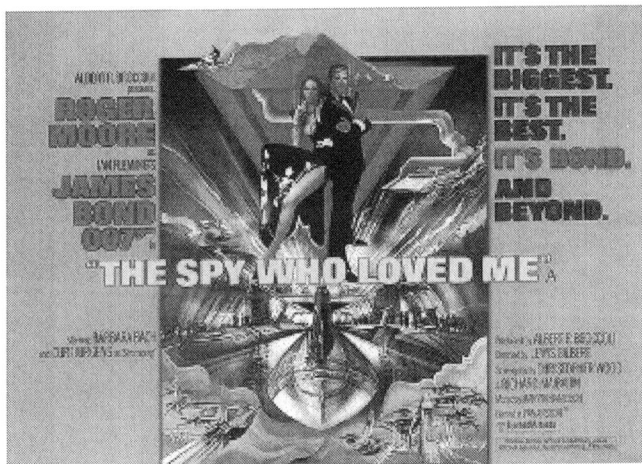

1977 saw James Bond 007 return to our screens in *The Spy Who Loved Me* – a spectacular caper starring Roger Moore (1927-2017) in his third outing as Bond.

The film opens with a breathtaking sequence where the secret agent skis off a cliff, saved at the last minute by a parachute bearing the Union Flag. Bond is then summoned to investigate the dissappearance of British and Soviet nuclear submarines.

Working in tandem with his Soviet counterpart, the beautiful Agent Triple X (Barbara Bach), Bond visits Egypt where he encounters the terrifying assassin, Jaws (Richard Kiel).

The disappearing subs are finally traced to Sardinia, in the secret underwater base of megalomaniac Karl Stromberg (Curt Jurgens). Stromberg is planning to destroy humanity and build a new civilization underwater.

Bond kills Stromberg, destroys the base and frees the captive submariners. He is finally discovered in bed with Agent Triple X by their respective superior officers, and insists that he is just 'keeping the British end up.'

Gay News on trial

First blasphemy prosecution since 1922

Moral campaigner Mary Whitehouse

The magazine *Gay News* in 1976 published a controversial poem by James Kirkup, *The Love That Dares To Speak Its Name*, which describes sexual encounters with Jesus.

The following year, media campaigner Mary Whitehouse took *Gay News* to court with a charge of blasphemous libel, an offence for which there had not been a similar trial for many years. The defence case was that the poem was about 'the universality of God's love', but Mrs Whitehouse said it was 'the recrucifixion of Christ by 20th-century weapons'.

Gay News lost the case, with the jury having a 10-2 majority.

The paper was fined and its editor, Denis Lemon, given a nine month prison sentence, which was suspended.

It was a landmark case, being the first successful prosecution for blasphemy in the United Kingdom since 1922. Public opinion was divided on the case, with many feeling it was an attack on free speech using outmoded laws no longer suited to contemporary society. Others felt it was a victory in the fight against declining moral values.

Blasphemy law was largely abolished in England, Wales and Scotland in 1998, although it remains in force in Northern Ireland.

Gary Powers killed

U2 test pilot dies in helicopter crash

Former U2 spyplane test pilot Gary Powers was involved in two air crashes in mysterious circumstances – the first he survived, but the second, on August 1 1977, was to prove fatal.

Powers, (born 1929) hit the headlines in 1960 when the high altitude U2 spy plane he was flying was shot down by a Russian missile. Powers, however, managed to use his ejector seat and on landing was captured and held by Soviet forces until 1962.

The US was forced to admit that the plane had been flying over Russian territory and entered into negotiations for the release of Powers; a process which was the subject of the 2015 thriller *Bridge of Spies.*

Powers was criticised for not having pressed the aircraft's self-destruct button to avoid it falling into Russian hands, and for not using a suicide capsule he had been ordered to take should he be captured.

Gary Powers in 1960

He was later exonerated, but his capture was, and continues to be, the subject of conspiracy theories, as does his eventual death in a helicopter crash over Los Angeles while working as a radio traffic reporter. The National Transportation Safety Board, however, attributed the accident to Powers' misreading of a faulty fuel gauge.

In 2012 Powers was posthumously awarded the Silver Star for gallantry in recognition of the suffering he endured during imprisonment in Russia.

Ford's big little car

The Fiesta appears on British roads

Although launched the previous year, the new Ford Fiesta did not appear on British roads until early in 1977. The car was Ford's answer to the burgeoning supermini class, and a contender with rivals such as the Fiat 127 and Renault 5.

Originally conceived as the 'Bobcat' in 1972, the Fiesta was produced in Spain, France, and Dagenham in the UK. The car was also made for the American market, beginning in 1978.

The car was initially available in 957 and 1117 cc engine sizes, Ghia trim and a van format. Later models included a 1.3l sports version and a Tuareg off roader.

In an era of rising fuel prices and shrinking urban parking spaces, the little Fiesta was a great success for Ford and, following various incarnations, is still in production forty years later, outliving all the other cars in its class, such as the long vanished Talbot Sunbeam and Austin Mini Metro.

Rudolf Stricker/Kieran White

The King is Dead

Elvis Presley, King of Rock and Roll, dies aged 42

Presley's grave at Graceland

The world of rock and roll was plunged into mourning when it learned of the death of its 'King', Elvis Presley, who suffered a fatal heart attack on 16 August 1977 at his home in Memphis, Tennessee.

Presley had been suffering from ill health for some years, and had found his touring schedule increasingly difficult to keep up with. His final single, *Way Down*, was released on 6 June and he performed his last concert in Indianapolis on 26 June.

Presley's funeral was held at his home, Graceland, on 18 August. A huge crowd of around 80,000 people jostled to see the procession, and in the confusion two women were killed when a car hit the crowd. A further incident marred Presley's passing; an attempt to steal his body in late August resulted in his grave being moved from Forest Hill Cemetery into the grounds of Graceland.

Presley's legacy was enormous: President Carter stated that he had 'permanently changed the face of American popular culture', with John Lennon adding later, 'before Elvis, there was nothing'.

Now, Voyager

Probe begins journey into deep space

Earth is still receiving signals from *Voyager 2*, a space probe which is now one of the furthest man-made objects from our world.

The probe was launched on 20 August 1977, a few days before its twin, *Voyager 1*. Its first destination was Jupiter, which was reached in 1979, and then Saturn, Uranus and Neptune, which it reached in 1989. It is now on an extended mission to explore the outer reaches of the solar system, and is now operating in interstellar space (the area between solar systems).

Although it sent back its last photos in 1990, the probe is still broadcasting radio signals to NASA's Deep Space Network, and is expected to have sufficient battery life to do so until 2020.

Left: equipment on *Voyager 2*. Below: artist's impression of the probe in space

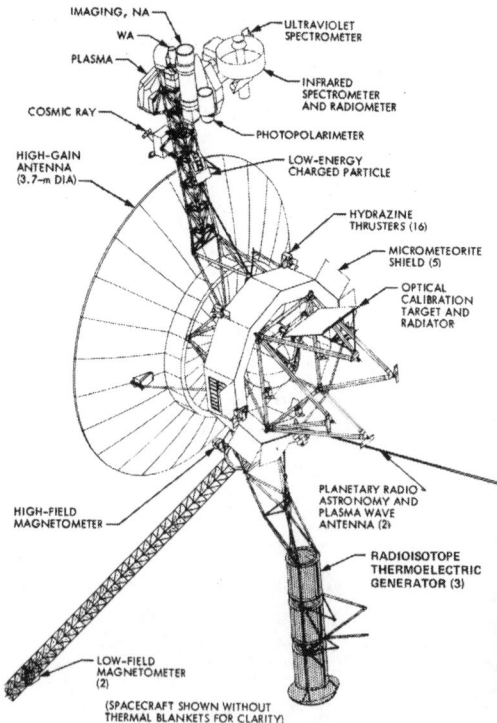

IMAGING, NA
WA
PLASMA
COSMIC RAY
HIGH-GAIN ANTENNA (3.7-m DIA)
ULTRAVIOLET SPECTROMETER
INFRARED SPECTROMETER AND RADIOMETER
PHOTOPOLARIMETER
LOW-ENERGY CHARGED PARTICLE
HYDRAZINE THRUSTERS (16)
MICROMETEORITE SHIELD (5)
OPTICAL CALIBRATION TARGET AND RADIATOR
PLANETARY RADIO ASTRONOMY AND PLASMA WAVE ANTENNA (2)
RADIOISOTOPE THERMOELECTRIC GENERATOR (3)
HIGH-FIELD MAGNETOMETER
LOW-FIELD MAGNETOMETER (2)
(SPACECRAFT SHOWN WITHOUT THERMAL BLANKETS FOR CLARITY)

All Time High

Russian plane breaks altitude record

A MiG-25 'Foxbat' similar to that used to break the world altitude record.

While American probes were aiming beyond the outer reaches of the solar system in 1977, Russian aircraft were attempting to break records closer to home, by flying a conventional aircraft at the highest altitude possible.

This was of obvious interest to governments wanting to carry out covert surveillance out of the reach of other aircraft or surface to air missiles. But at high altitude the air eventually becomes so thin it becomes impossible for a plane's wings to sustain flight, making such journeys a highly risky activity.

On 31 August 1977, Chief Test Pilot Alexander Fedotov reached 123,520 ft (23.44 miles) in a modified Mikoyan-Gurevich MiG-25 'Foxbat' jet fighter over Podmoskovnoye in the USSR.

Fedotov had also broken the previous world altitude record in 1973, narrowly escaping disaster when his engines cut out due to the thinness of the air.

The guillotine's final fall

The last execution in France

Convicted killer Hamida Djandoubi (above) was the last man to be executed in France, beheaded by the guillotine (inset).

Tunisian immigrant Hamida Djandoubi (1949-1977) was sentenced to death on 25 February 1977 for the murder of 22 year old Élisabeth Bousquet in Marseille, whom he tortured and killed after she refused to work for him as a prostitute.

Following a final unsuccessful appeal for mercy to President Valéry Giscard d'Estaing, Djandoubi was executed by the guillotine at 4.40 am on 10 September 1977.

The guillotine, infamous for its widespread use in the Terror following the French Revolution in 1789, caused instant death by decapitation. Use of the device was abolished along with the death penalty in France in 1981 under the government of François Mitterrand.

In addition to being the last man executed in France, Djandoubi remains the last person to be legally executed in the European Union.

Marc Bolan killed

T-Rex frontman dies in car crash

In addition to Elvis Presley the music world lost another legend in 1977: glam rock icon Marc Bolan of T-Rex, who died in a car accident aged just 29.

Born in east London, Bolan showed early musical promise when joined a school skiffle band in the early 1960s, performing with vocalist Helen Shapiro. Later he was part of the band John's Children but did not achieve real fame until forming glam-rock band T-Rex in 1967. Their single, *Ride a White Swan* peaked in 1971 at number two in the charts.

Its success was followed by other chart-topping hits including *Get it On* and *Hot Love.*

Tragedy struck in the early hours of 16 September as Bolan travelled home from central London in a 1275 GT Mini driven by friend Gloria Jones. Jones lost control of the vehicle which hit a tree in the suburb of Barnes. Jones was injured but Bolan was killed instantly.

The spot where he died (below left) has become a shrine for fans from all over the world.

Britmax

All aboard the Skytrain!

Budget airline slashes fares to New York

If you think budget airlines started with Easyjet, think again! In 1977 the Skytrain service began flights from London to New York at the staggeringly low cost of £59, about one third of the cost of major competitors.

Skytrain was the brainchild of aviation entrepreneur Sir Frederick 'Freddie' Laker (1922-2006) who in 1971 proposed a budget transatlantic airline. There was stiff opposition from established carriers who did not want prices to be lowered, and in 1975 Laker fought the British government in court after his aviation licence was revoked. Following intervention by US President Carter, Skytrain finally went into service on 26 September 1977 on the Gatwick-JFK route.

It was hugely popular at first, with other airlines matching the low fares, but eventually went into administration in 1982 following a series of setbacks.

Laker's lasting legacy was his influence on other airline entrepreneurs such as Sir Richard Branson (Virgin) and Sir Stelios Haji-Ioannou (Easyjet).

Pelé has left the pitch

Soccer legend retires

Football legend Edson Arantes do Nascimento (known simply as Pelé) played his final professional game on 1 October 1977 – playing for both sides!

Pelé, thought by many to be the greatest ever footballer, was born in 1940 and began his career with Brazilian team Santos at 15, moving on to the national side a year later.

During his international career, he won three FIFA World Cups: 1958, 1962 and 1970, being the only player ever to do so. Pelé remains the all-time leading goalscorer for Brazil with 77 goals in 92 games.

Although his last international game took place in 1971, his final match was a friendly between New York Cosmos and Santos. The match was played in front of a sold-out crowd at Giants Stadium and was televised in the United States on ABC's *Wide World of Sports.*

Pelé played the first half for the Cosmos and the second half for Santos. Pelé scored his final goal from a direct free kick, and Cosmos won 2–1.

'That was a great game of golf, fellas'

Bing Crosby dies

White Christmas singer Bing Crosby died following a golf game on 13 October 1977.

The veteran star of swing music and movies shot to fame in the 1930s and became one of the highest paid entertainers of his era. He released 396 chart singles, 41 of which were number ones.

Based on ticket sales, he is the third most popular cinema actor of all time, after Clark Gable and John Wayne; his 'Road' movies with Bob Hope were particularly popular. In his final year the star visited the UK and in his last TV appearance (a prerecorded Christmas show) he performed his now famous duet, *Little Drummer Boy,* with David Bowie. His last public concert was in Brighton on 10 October.

Following a pleasant day's golfing while holidaying in Spain, the singer collapsed and died instantly. His last words to his fellow players are reputed to have been 'That was a great game of golf, fellas.'

Fire dispute heats up

National strike by fire brigade

Firemen across the UK came out on strike on 14 November 1977. Unions demanded a 30% pay increase but the government would not move beyond 10%; the unions settled in for a long struggle.

Troops provided cover, often insufficiently trained and equipped with outdated technology such as 1950s Green Goddess fire engines, kept in reserve after the disbanding of the volunteer Auxiliary Fire Service in 1968. Soldiers averted a major catastrophe on Merseyside when they stopped a haulage depot blaze at Kirkdale spreading to a 500-gallon petrol storage tank.

Some firefighters did break the strike, particularly during a fire at St Andrew's hospital in London. The strike continued until 12 January 1978.

Below: Royal Marines with a 1950s Green Goddess Auxiliary Fire Service engine.

Elliot Simpson

Mull of Kintyre

Wings hit is Christmas number one

Above: the Mull of Kintyre with Northern Ireland in the distance. Inset: Paul McCartney.

Ex-Beatle Paul McCartney and his band Wings had a Christmas number one in 1977 with the song *Mull of Kintyre.*

The recording spent nine weeks at the top of the charts and went on to become the first single to sell over two million copies in Britain, making it the best selling UK single of all time, until it was overtaken by Band Aid's *Do They Know It's Christmas* in 1984.

Paul McCartney described how the song came about:

I certainly loved Scotland enough, so I came up with a song about where we were living: an area called Mull of Kintyre. It was a love song really, about how I enjoyed being there and imagining I was travelling away and wanting to get back there.

The Mull of Kintyre is an area on the west coast of Scotland with outstanding views of Northern Ireland. Unusually, McCartney's vocals and guitar playing were recorded outdoors, and the song featured a local pipe band from Campbeltown.

Saturday Night Fever

Disco movie is smash hit

Saturday Night Fever, starring John Travolta, was one of the top five grossing films of 1977.

With its thumping disco soundtrack mainly by the Bee Gees, the film tells the story of New Yorker Tony Manero, who works in a dead end job by day but who spends his nights in dancing competitions at discotheques.

Although the film is very much a period piece, it has remained popular largely due to the numerous hit songs performed in it, including *How Deep is Your Love, Stayin' Alive, Night Fever, More than a Woman, Jive Talking* and *Disco Inferno.*

Somewhat unusually, the film was reissued two years later in an expurgated form with bad language removed and some scenes reshot to make it more suitable for teenagers who had enjoyed the soundtrack album, but who were not allowed to see the original film in cinemas.

The film catapulted the young little-known actor John Travolta to stardom.

Aged 24, he also became one of the youngest actors to be nominated for an Academy Award, third only to child stars Jackie Cooper and Mickey Rooney.

Journey's end for the 'Tramp'

Charlie Chaplin dies aged 88

On Christmas Day 1977, Sir Charles Spencer 'Charlie' Chaplin KBE died at his home in Switzerland, one of the last living links with the Victorian world of music hall (vaudeville) comedy.

Born in poverty in south London to a mentally unstable mother and alcoholic father, Chaplin spent time as a child in a workhouse, (the state institution for the destitute).

As a child Chaplin supported himself by performing dances and comedy routines on the stages of the music halls, the main form of public entertainment for the masses in the days before cinema. He was spotted by empresario Fred Karno and began his rise to fame, particularly after moving to the USA and making his first movie in 1914 for slapstick king Mack Sennett. Chaplin's 'Tramp' character became wildly popular and assured him a place in cinema history.

With the arrival of the 'talkies' Chaplin began to adapt to more serious films and despite being exiled from the USA for his political views, he continued as an actor and director in Europe into the 1960s.

Chaplin with co-star Edna Purviance in 1915.

BIRTHDAY NOTEBOOKS

FROM
MONTPELIER PUBLISHING

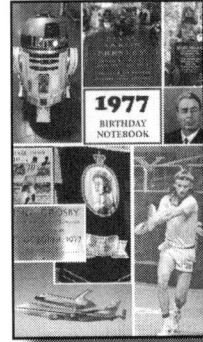

Handy 60-page ruled notebooks with a significant event of the year on each page.

A great alternative to a birthday card.
Available from Amazon.

Printed in Great Britain
by Amazon